SLASHING SOUNDS

T0182236

PHOENIX POETS
Edited by Srikanth Reddy
Rosa Alcalá, Douglas Kearney &
Katie Peterson, consulting editors

Slashing Sounds

A Bilingual Edition

JOLANDA INSANA
TRANSLATED BY CATHERINE THEIS

THE UNIVERSITY OF CHICAGO PRESS

CHICAGO & LONDON

The University of Chicago Press, Chicago 60637
The University of Chicago Press, Ltd., London
Fendenti fonici ©1982 by Società di poesia, Milano; 2007 by Garzanti, Milano
Translation ©2024 by Catherine Theis
Published 2024
Printed in the United States of America

33 32 31 30 29 28 27 26 25 24   1 2 3 4 5

ISBN-13: 978-0-226-83574-7 (paper)
ISBN-13: 978-0-226-83575-4 (e-book)
DOI: https://doi.org/10.7208/chicago/9780226835754.001.0001

Library of Congress Cataloging-in-Publication Data

Names: Insana, Jolanda, 1937–2016, author. | Theis, Catherine, translator. | Insana, Jolanda, 1937–
    2016. Fendenti fonici. | Insana, Jolanda, 1937–2016. Fendenti fonici. English.
Title: Slashing sounds : a bilingual edition / Jolanda Insana ; translated by Catherine Theis.
Other titles: Phoenix poets.
Description: Chicago : The University of Chicago Press, 2024. | Series: Phoenix poets | Includes
    bibliographical references. | Parallel text in Italian and English.
Identifiers: LCCN 2024008407 | ISBN 9780226835747 (paperback) | ISBN 9780226835754 (ebook)
Subjects: LCGFT: Poetry.
Classification: LCC PQ4869.N77 F4613 2024 | DDC 851/.914—dc23/eng/20240401
LC record available at https://lccn.loc.gov/2024008407

♾ This paper meets the requirements of ANSI/NISO Z39.48-1992 (Permanence of Paper).

for Gianluca

CONTENTS

TRANSLATOR'S NOTE

Some things could only be written in a foreign language;
they are not lost in translation, but conceived by it.

> SVETLANA BOYM, "Estrangement as a Lifestyle: Shklovsky and Brodsky"

1

Suppose one is a translator. Perhaps the job is well-suited for those who prefer plunging, falling, sinking, plummeting, diving, dropping, or descending to the core of some ecstatic or infernal abyss.

Here you won't find a neat treatise on translation. I won't discuss a translation in terms of its fidelities or failures. I don't concern myself with the question of originals. I won't bore you with theories regarding a work's afterlife or metaphoric growth. A definitive definition of translation doesn't exist. Each act of translation depends upon its context; much like a live performance, it cannot be repeated. Although the script and actors may be the same, no two shows, or texts, are ever identical.

2

Jolanda Insana writes:

> gorgeous rich and rogue
> is my ideal of a poet.

I couldn't agree more.

3

Jolanda Insana (1937–2016) was a Sicilian poet. Born in Messina, Insana moved to Rome after graduating from the University of Messina, where she wrote a thesis on Erinna's *The Distaff*, an ancient elegy for the poet's friend Baucis. In Rome she taught classical literature to high school students, translated Greek and Latin poetry, and wrote her own poems. Insana's first published poems, collectively titled *Sciarra amara*, appeared in 1977 in an edited volume that featured other poets as well. Filled with images from Sicily's puppet theater, her contribution employs archaic forms and dialect to explore the universal themes of life and death.

Fendenti fonici, which I have translated as *Slashing Sounds*, is Insana's first full collection and the first book-length edition of her work in English. The poems are composed of between nine and twenty-one short numbered sections. Pulsing with the growl of Sicilian language, this collection uses invectives, fragments, epigrams, and epigraphs to achieve a unified work that resembles a total poem. Her preoccupation with language—with words heard first as patterned sound— endears me to her larger conception of poetry as a voiced anima. Insana won the Viareggio Prize for poetry for *La stortura* in 2002 and the Premio Pascoli di Poesia in 2009.

4

In "Noose Soaked in Orange Blossom Water," Insana writes:

> my word
> word of poetry
> an ongoing immoral parliament
> between the great assembly and the merchants
>
> is it better to be stone or terra-cotta pitcher?

I am both stone and terra-cotta pitcher. My father is American; my mother is Italian. I grew up speaking Italian—Sicilian, really—though I didn't learn how to read or write until I was in college. I was embarrassed by this fact. Italian was my first language, but I never thought that I should translate it. Surely there were more qualified people. But as time went on, I realized how much I longed for some part of me that was submerged, missing, muted. If I'm honest, the impulse to translate Italian poems stemmed from a desire to hear old voices, to replay what was said around me in the hope of remembering moments from my childhood and all the people I loved and missed. I started reading more poetry in Italian beyond Dante. But all the Italian poems I read (think Montale and Ungaretti) sounded too stately, too removed from my own experiences in Italy. Their beauty and abstraction left me restless, careless.

A thoughtful teacher intuited who and what I was looking for. He handed me Insana's collected poems, a lovely fat turquoise paperback. "These are hard," he said. "But she's Sicilian. Have a look." What I find arresting in Insana's work is her commitment to contentiousness, her brutal and skeptical eye, and above all, her preoccupation with language. There is no subject more worthy of our interest than language's misfires, its abuses, and its contradictory impulses—language being the ultimate arrow or sword, a direction in the world, a turn toward whatever reality appears in front of you. In her poems, there is repetition, bouts of madness. "I take care of my nothings" is something I might've said or hoped to say in one of my more illuminating moments of self-awareness. As readers we are drawn to voices that remind us of our past lives or encounters, our shadow selves.

5

Translation is always both possible and impossible. The untranslatable exists alongside or within the translated—it is why we keep on translating. What's said in one language can be said in another. Translation is not loss; it is joyful accumulation, indebted to the highs and lows of the translator's peregrinations around the untranslated.

Many practitioners maintain that the art of translation is fueled by the in-between moments—grocery shopping, caregiving, or sleeping—when untranslated words and phrases suddenly reveal themselves in the other language. This is true of my practice. How many times have I driven to the store with a poem pinned to my lapel just to have it close, only to pull over on the side of the road, rip it off, and make a note in blue ink when an idea seizes me, pushing me in a direction I wasn't expecting? Translation's impossibility requires attendance, but it's not enough to simply show up.

If there's anything I wish to say about translation, it's that translation relies on a triangular system of dailiness, abundance, and performance. It is a friendship, a constellation, a rigged-up circuit, a cast-iron sieve panning for gold. Translation is an active encounter. As Sandra Bermann argues, when we perform a translation, we are asked to inhabit two worlds, then to reconcile their difference ("Performing Translation," in *A Companion to Translation Studies*, ed. Sandra Bermann and Catherine Porter [Hoboken, NJ: Wiley, 2014], 293). It coaxes out a sense of continuity, a shared history from distinct experiences. It is a confrontation with otherness. Translation wonders, How might the individual artist make sense of her commitments to the work, to herself, and to her larger cultural and political communities?

Here is Insana describing her own translation process: "Translation is not only an extraordinary exercise or entrance into another's workshop—it is, above all, a beautiful technique of courtship and a nearing of the poet whose word you believe to be true and natural; it feigns to overcome the distance and yet communicates every difference in time, place, and things. In short, it is a body-to-body loving, arousal and discovery, a respect for the identity of others, not forgetting that the other is and always remains other" ("Parlare di poesia?," in *Voci e silenzi: la re-visione al femminile nella poesia di lingua inglese*, ed. Vita Fortunati and Gabriella Morisco [Urbino: Quattroventi, 1993], 193–94; my translation).

Insana acknowledges the negotiation of difference, a reconciliation of the highest order, as something wildly transformative. I mention this reading of translation because performance is also important to her original poetry. Insana's poems meditate upon and often employ metaphors from Sicilian marionette theater, and her peculiar poetic language springs from the stage's preoccupation with representation and reality. In fact, she represents her poems as a kind of microtheater, one that is itself a metaphor for life. In her *teatrino* ("little theater"), the poet is both the puppet and puppeteer. At the beginning of *Sciarra amara*, the speaker says, "I am a puppet / and build a theater with only two puppets / her and her / she's called life / and she's called death" ("Pupara sono," in *Quaderni della Fenice 26* [Milan: Guanda, 1977], lines 1–5; my translation). The two puppets are, of course, the speaker herself. This exchange between life and death sets the scene for the rest of Insana's work, in which she never forgets the other and dramatizes how all life is a constant negotiation between pleasure and pain. In *Slashing Sounds*, the poems are neorealistic, expressive, and cemented in sound. They are about language, how it rips and carries itself across the speaking parts, as illustrated in the violence of a speaker who casually suggests, "you could try a snip-snip / of hidden threads and pushed-down puppets."

Insana uses her knowledge of classical languages to corrupt her poetry. For example, here's the opening to "An Old Pleasure":

> the sticky shitmarker
> scammy scoundrel
> making chatterings chitchat and lies
> encloses his realm of nonsense
> by bellowing at bellycrawlers
> with fairytales of piping-hot boiled meats
> and boiled lexemes
>
> it's fated for Christ's sake to cast slashing sounds.

Emanuele Broccio argues that "the sound in Insana's work is already substance, deep core" ("Jolanda Insana: una lingua per scuotere le menti," *Mantichora* 8 [2018]: 135; my translation). In other words, her pressure on language, the bubbling and the boiling, begins an alchemical process, a transmutation of matter, whereby poetry breathes sacred air.

6

Repeated words, like "bile," "blows," and "bitterness," appear against a Roman land-scape, somewhere between the Senate building and the poetry factory. Other words, like "nails," "kicks," and "punches," conjure a dangerous battlefield. The speaker's body becomes the battlefield, pocked and scarred by the blows of rocks, nails, and other bodies. War, a war from which we never return, is often the backdrop. At war are the Sicilian and Italian tongues. The southern dialect rears its proverbial ugly head as the visceral language, the one closer to bodily functions and the lyrical self, while echoes of a Dantean vernacular blend with standard Italian. There are also traces of ancient Greek and Latin—lamentations, aphorisms, and wisdom. I have left the Latin phrases untranslated in the English text but have provided a glossary (see page 79). These competing registers of language create a polyphonic voice. Because of this, Broccio reads Insana as a plurilingual poet. Her poetry is deeply influenced by her translations of Sappho, Euripides, and Andreas Cappellanus, and she traces her lineage back to the corrupt Dante, leaving Petrarch's perfection in the dust. In the poem "Another Loss of Speech," the speaker says,

> the words however mean everything
> and they speak to me from the center
> not from outside or from around.

7

Why does anyone translate? To spot the other in the self. To call out difference. To amass gigantic piles of notes, endnotes, blueprints, lectures, graphs, systems, tunnels, walkways, rivers, landscapes of pitted feeling and pocked history—all to be used in a later procession. To clothe books. To be defiant. To realize our preoccupations and obsessions have run parallel with others' at different moments in history. To spot likeness. To practice, to write, to subscribe. To attend. To choose life over death.

SLASHING SOUNDS

partiamo per la guerra dei meloni
nessuno torna alla sua dimora

*

we leave for the war of the melons
nobody returns home

Niente dissi

1

di referenze ne ho assai
più di quanto basta

2

il referente sono io
e me ne vanto

3

mi specchio e sgravo con dolore
figliando famiglie di parole
immagini pargolette e sorelline maggiori

lo specchio sono io
sono io il mio stesso io
e tu ci sformi

4

fuori dello specchio
avanti la mia comparsa
non ci furono prepensieri né presentimenti
mentre tu credi d'esserci tu

narciso per narciso ti giuro
che sono io narcisa e crisostoma

5

io mi faccio come mi pare e piace
fuori e dentro il mondo
per beccherie osterie e giochi d'artificio

qualche volta mi lascio fare
e allora sì che sono guai

I Said Nothing

1

I have a lot of references
more than enough

2

the referent is me
and I'm proud of it

3

I mirror myself and spawn with pain
forming families of words
baby pictures and older little sisters

the mirror is me
it's me my true self
and you are disturbed by it

4

out of the mirror
in front of my appearance
there weren't any premonitions or presentiments
while you believe you're here

narcissus for narcissus I swear
that I'm narcisa and goldmund

5

I invent myself as I like
outside and inside the world
through butcher shops taverns and fireworks

sometimes I let myself go
and then yes there's trouble

6

però non scappo anche se ci fu un tempo
che mi fecero scappare per arcadie salotti e sacrestie
ma non ero io
la poesia
era la pallida e sminchiata ombra mia

7

e comunque non mi piscio
né mi scrivo addosso
è lui che pretende d'inscriversi in me
e ingravidarmi tutta quanta come vacca
non escludo che una volta su dieci riesce
a rovesciarmi in testa i suoi pitali
e a farmi girare le sue frittate

fino a quando però non mi girano le palle
e al poeta glielo dico io
culus perforatus non habet dominum

8

de malo in malum
tornat et retornat
male dormit poeta qui non manducat

9

ma se vuole manducare de lacte et pane bono
suam vaccam debet nutrire

10

invece più d'una volta
e non ti so dire quante
il ruffiano pennivendolo
mi svacca a morire

planta de genista revertitur ad scopam
e non sempre scopa nova fa gran sfruscio

6

but I don't escape even if there was a time
when they made me run through arcades salons and sacristies
but it wasn't me
poetry
was my pale and limp shadow

7

and in any case I don't piss
or write on myself
he's the one who demands to inscribe himself on me
and knocks me all up like a cow
I'm not ruling out that one in ten times he manages
to dump his bedpans over my head
and turns it around on me

until he busts my balls
and I say to the poet
culus perforatus non habet dominum

8
de malo in malum
tornat et retornat
male dormit poeta qui non manducat

9
but if he wants to eat de lacte et pane bono
suam vaccam debet nutrire

10
instead more than once
and I can't say how many times
the pimp writer hack
leaves me to die

planta de genista revertitur ad scopam
and a new broom doesn't always make a great rustle

11

e poi non basta lo sfruscio
il nome e la nomea
ci vuole qualcosa d'altro
altrimenti davvero sbianca e piange
pure l'inanimata scavatrice

12

se c'ero non c'ero
se non c'ero ci sono

13

niente vidi
niente so
niente dissi
e se dissi niente
dissi tutto

14

de cultello ad pistolam
de cucina ad cessum
de ovo ad gallinam
de scala ad montem
de schola ad ecclesiam

15

e poi mi permetto di mettere il cappello
a chi non ha capo

16

chi non ha capo
mi toglie cappello e berretta
mi storce la coppola
mi strappa le braghe
mi lascia col culo di fuori
mi scopre i genitali e ci sputa sopra

11

the rustle the name and the reputation
it's not enough
you need something else
otherwise even the lifeless digger
really goes pale and cries

12

if I was there I wasn't there
if I wasn't there I'm here

13

I saw nothing
I know nothing
I said nothing
and if I said nothing
I said everything

14

de cultello ad pistolam
de cucina ad cessum
de ovo ad gallinam
de scala ad montem
de schola ad ecclesiam

15

and then let me put the hat
on those who have no head

16

headless
he pulls off my hat and cap
tears off my beret
rips off my pants
leaves me with my ass hanging out
the pig that he is

il porco che è lui
sogguarda la pisella che è una bellapisella
e dice
ecco lo dicevo non è pura
che vergogna

17
s'incappuccia tutto grinzoso
in un sacco stravecchio
e pretende da me risposta
non altro germinando

ma quale risposta alla strazzosa pecoraggine

18
allevata in un paese ruvido e selvaggio
ho per amanti
teneruzzi e ruvidazzi
poveri scannati di fame e golosìa
che mi tengono di sopra
stretta per gli stretti fianchi
e ci sussurriamo cose che non si vendono
e si devono donare

chi non ha manco ragione
grida forte e ricatta in nome mio
i miei amanti amano il triccheballacco dell'ironia

19
e a chi mi vuole spogliare svergognare
e spubblicare
io dico
ti do la lana non la pecora

finds my genitals and spits on them
eyes the cherry that is a beautiful cherry
and says
look I told you it wasn't pure
what a disgrace

17
he hoods himself all wrinkled
in an old worn-out sack
and demands answers from me
giving life to nothing else

but how to respond to such stupidity

18
raised in a rough and savage town
I have as lovers
sweethearts and ruffians
poor men butchered by hunger and gluttony
who hold me on top
tight on my skinny sides
and we whisper things that can't be sold
and must be given away

those who have no reason
scream loudly and blackmail in my name
my lovers love the tambourine of irony

19
and whoever wants to strip me to shame
and dismiss me
I say
I give you the wool not the sheep

Un vecchio piacere

1

il cacasegni sticchioso
risbaldo rubaldo
facendo ciarlamenti frappe e bugie
recinge il suo regno di balordìa
per bettolare a tirapancia
con favolatori di lessi bollenti
e lessemi bolliti

è giocoforza perdìo dare fendenti fonici

2

scialate-scialate
rattoppatori di cenci raccattonati
prima o poi arriva il giubileo mengaldo
che depone croce de profundis et de sanctis

3

persa la carta di navigazione
vanno trappoliando per feste asinarie
tra molisi e martinefranche
i poveretti che fanno tricchetracche
e tanto a parte

ma pesce di cannuccia resta pesce di cannuccia

4

per conto mio non voglio fare la fine
di quel tale che per non dire bè
si pigliò trent'anni di galera

5

c'è nell'aria un vecchio piacere
—prendere il cielo a calci e pugni
e mozzicarsi i coglioni

An Old Pleasure

1

the sticky shitmarker
scammy scoundrel
making chatterings chitchat and lies
encloses his realm of nonsense
by bellowing at bellycrawlers
with fairytales of piping-hot boiled meats
and boiled lexemes

it's fated for Christ's sake to cast slashing sounds

2

live it up whoop it up
patchworks of collected rags
sooner or later the mengaldo jubilee arrives
that lays down croce de profundis et de sanctis

3

they lost the map
they go trapping for feasts of asses
between molise and martina franca
the poor guys who turn tricks
besides so much else

but naive people remain naive

4

and I don't want to end up
like that guy who didn't say a word yeah well
he got thirty years in jail

5

there's an old pleasure in the air
—taking out the sky with kicks and punches
and cutting off your balls

io infuoco la posta
in questo gioco che mi strazia
e punto forte sulla carta

6
te la puoi salare la tua lingua
non mi mette né freddo né febbre

7
sarò lagnosa ma non mi scordo
di quel che bolle in pentola
e come si crepa d'agosto sotto una pensilina
e così ti avviso et armo
poeta

8
non mi passa per la capa
metterti la testa ai piedi
ma vorrei che tu e io uscissimo dall'incantamento
per vedere dove camminano i poveretti
come stanno stinnicchiati i morti e gli ammazzati
quanto costa il pane sciapo
e il coraggio di dire «fuori dal tempio i mercanti»
dappoiché a casa di Pilato chi è orbo e chi è sciancato

9
e poi non rubare
le altrui braghe rompono il culo
gli altrui topoi rosicano la carta

10
non serve avere le mani in pasta
ci vuole farina e acqua
penna e carta
per non dare al diavolo l'anima e la crusca

I up the ante
in this game that torments me
and bet high on the card

6
you can salt your speech
neither cold nor fever sits well with me

7
I will be cranky but I won't forget
what's brewing in the pot
and how you die in august waiting for the bus
and so you are warned and armed
poet

8
it doesn't cross my mind
to put my head at your feet
but I would like for you and me to leave the enchantment
to see where the poor guys walk
how the dead and the murdered are splayed out
how much the unsalted bread costs
and the courage to say "the merchants outside of the temple"
since those who are one-eyed and maimed are at Pilate's house

9
and besides don't steal
other people's pants break your ass
other places chew the paper

10
no need to have hands in dough
it takes flour and water
pen and paper
not to give spirit and husk to the devil

Un'altra afasia

1

tu no
qualcun altro però me prende a ore
mi sbatte
pronto con un piede nelle staffe
a correre in fureria
si sbatte anche lui un po' in verità
e poi si vanta d'essere l'amante mio
gli piacerebbe poveretto
ma io non ho peli sulla lingua
e gli dico zozzò-zozzò in altra albergherìa
non fare il poeta del cazzo
(anche perché cazzo è bello

2

turucturo fame che fame kaora-kaora
sono una carnavala spacchiata e spacciata
mi lasciano la parola e tolgono la comunicazione
è come prima
è un'altra afasia

3

ho spalle forti per portare la realtà che pesa
non uso fantasmi
non parlo per interposta persona
non mi fido di compari e comparoni
e dirò con la mia voce mia
l'espropriazione che nei secoli ho subìto

so d'essere dimezzata
ma te lo dico io
senza fole né inganni

Another Loss of Speech

1

you no
but someone else takes me by the hour
bangs me up
ready with one foot in the stirrups
to run to the orderly's room
in truth he bangs himself up a bit
and then boasts of being my lover
the poor man would like that
but I don't mince words
and I tell him chop-chop to another inn
don't be a fucking poet
(also because fucking is beautiful

2

drone hunger that hungers hot-hot
I am a carnival blasted and blissful
even damaged goods have the last word
it's like before
it's another loss of speech

3

I have strong shoulders to carry weighty reality
I don't use ghosts
I don't speak through third parties
I don't trust homies or cronies
and I will tell with my own voice
the expropriation I have suffered over the centuries

I know I'm half of myself
but I will tell you
without tales or deception

4

sbramando d'essere acratica
non ho capito bene
non ho deciso ancora
se la lingua mi lascia dire
o mi obbliga

5

comunque le parole significano tutto
e mi parlano dal centro
non di fuori né d'intorno

6

io voglio essere e sono con crudelezza
quello che segno
non voglio simboleggiare

via la sacralità
è un modo antico per tapparmi la bocca e fottermi ancora

7

non spunta giunco dove non c'è acqua
e sono oggetto di religione di beffa o d'ironia
perché senza soggetto e senza padri
piccolo o audace gioco di fantasia
e chissàcosasia

8

potessi essere reale
legittima con una madre e un padre regolari
non scambiabile con nessuna parafrasi o perifrasi

ma il fatto è che non sono un'altra cosa

4

desiring to be powerless
I didn't quite understand
I haven't yet decided
whether the tongue allows me to talk
or forces me to

5

the words however mean everything
and they speak to me from the center
not from outside or from around

6

I want to be and I am with cruelty
what I sign
I don't want to symbolize

away from the sacredness
it's an ancient way to shut me up and fuck me again

7

no reed grows where there's no water
and I'm the object of religion made from mockery or irony
because without a subject and without fathers
who knows what this is
this small or daring fantasy game

8

could I be real
legitimate with a regular mother and father
not interchangeable with any paraphrase or periphrasis

but the fact is I'm not another thing

9

e nel profilo di rischio entrano
adulatori mercanti in fiera grassatori
grassisàturi ventosità e tante amenità

c'è di che crepare scoppiando di bile e di parole

10

non importa se tu o altri
fa testamento e confessione
mangiando salsicce e maccaroni
augurando cancrena all'altrui mano

11

voglio rubare il cerchio dei bambini
e farlo girare a ruota libera
dove le strade sono più trafficate
e il pedone . . .

9
and they enter the risk profile
flatterers merchants at the fair robbers
saturated fats windiness and many amenities

there's enough to kick the bucket bursting with bile and words

10
it doesn't matter if you or others
draw up a will and confession
eating sausages and macaroni
wishing gangrene on someone else's hand

11
I want to steal the circle of children
and make it whirl and spin free
where the streets are the busiest
and the pedestrian . . .

Nessuna consolazione

1
nessuna consolazione
per questa sviolinata primavera
di femminei controcanti
ricacciati al fondo della gola
se voglio essere io
narciso senza specchio
e mi guardo intorno e scotto
e sputo fiele e getto fuoco dalle nasche

2
prima del dibattito
come soggetto parlante
senza il cappello dell'a-priori o del priore
voglio che si definisca il mio territorio
per non finire poi in una morsicatura d'api senza miele

3
se il femminile ti calza stretto
non capisco perché vuoi calzare me
tu che tieni in frigorifero le tue isterie

4
sei libero di dire e di pensare
che permutando il segno
innovi il rapporto con il reale e i suoi mutamenti

e se le parole fossero schioppettate?

5
bello ricco e malandrino
è il mio ideale di poeta
ma se si sminchia in mercatura di sacchi vuoti
acqua davanti vento di dietro
e sapone sotto i piedi

No Consolation

1

no consolation
for this brilliant spring
of feminine countermelodies
pushed to the bottom of the throat
if I want to be me
narcissus without a mirror
and look around and burn
and spit bile and spout fire from my nostrils

2

before the debate
as a speaking subject
without the hat of a priori or of prior
I would like to define my territory
so as to not end up with a bee sting without honey

3

if the feminine fits you tight
I don't understand why you want to fit me
you who keep your hysteria in the fridge

4

you are free to say and to think
that by swapping the sign
you innovate the relationship with reality and its changes

and what if the words were shot?

5

gorgeous rich and rogue
is my ideal of a poet
but if it turns into a business of empty bags
water in front wind in the back
and suds under the feet

6

non bramo pisciare fora dell'orinale
e non volendo essere tutto
mi attengo al mio niente
al mio svanimento di testa
per trarre un soggetto da un testo senza

7

e poi dovendo crepare
meglio della consunzione è un colpo secco
una mazzata tra le corna

non mi piace tirare le cuoia
con le scarpe ai piedi e il respire acido

8

ricacciata al fondo degli armadi
cenerentola delle collane editoriali
dovrei tenermi il torto e il morto

9

amante tua non amata
più che amante amata e poi tradita
con tutte le porcherie e soperchierie
che a nome mio si fanno
e quando voglio
ti lascio io

10

da quando in qua
il sale fa vermi?

11

sarà perché mi hai toccato il polso
che sanza tremore imbrachetti
tavole fuori testo

6

I don't long to piss outside of the urinal
and I don't want to be everyone
I take care of my nothings
my vanishing head
to draw a subject from an empty lyric

7

and then having to die
a sharp blow is better than consumption
a blow between the horns

I don't like to kick the bucket
with acid breath and my shoes on

8

pushed to the bottom of the cabinets
cinderella of the editorial series
I suffer double damage

9

your lover unloved
more than lover loved and then betrayed
with all the filth and abuse
done in my name
and when I want
the one who leaves you is me

10

since when does
salt make worms?

11

it is because you touched my wrist
that without trembling you bind
tables out of text

e imbrocchi strade d'innamoramento
braccandomi all'uscita

12
volendo non ho amore né sapore
so di poco e vivo come posso
finché non arriva lui
in gran dispitto
a farmi mangiare le ossa con il sale

13
e forse alle tue carte
preferisco la carta dei pazzi o dei carcerati
il muro bianco
contro vecchi e nuovi pronunciamenti

14
taci-e-maci
fra noi non c'è menzogna
e tu entri nelle altrui tane come il riccio
che aculeando sloggia-e-sloggia

15
non sono rose e fiori per nessuno
ho il fiato amaro
e non mi va di consolare
il lagno che schiuma come piscio

a questo patto e senza amarore
c'è ancora posto
altrimenti puoi farti la truscia
e cercare altrove la via del rifugio

16
forse il rosario
può esserti maestro e guida
nelle spine della vita

and cross streets of infatuation
stalking me at the exit

12
if desired I have no love nor taste
I taste of nothing and live how I can
until he gets here
with great scorn
to make me eat bones with salt

13
and maybe about your cards
I prefer the crazy or prisoner card
the white wall
against old and new pronouncements

14
silently face-to-face
between us there's no lie
and you enter the other lairs like a hedgehog
that ousts and ejects by pricking

15
I'm roses and flowers for nobody
I have bitter breath
and I'm inconsolable
the complaint that foams like piss

to this pact and without bitterness
there's still space
otherwise you can get the luggage
and look elsewhere for shelter

16
maybe the rosary
can be a teacher and guide
through the thorns of life

17
e comunque non sono pesce per la tua padella
friggi e soffriggi altri
io sono piccolo e nigro
e non basto alla tua gola

18
avrai poco tempo per dire
avanzando l'onda nera sul fiume
o tutto il tempo che vorrai
se ti fottono con la storia della mia eternità
non credere ai bugiardi e agli ottimisti
rivendica la tua libertà
di finire nei canali e nei pantani

19
sento che finirò olofrastica
o tornerò più indietro
alla lallazione

20
onestamente non posso dire
d'essere un cazzo furioso e confuso
anche se la testa la perdo anch'io

21
poesia o nonpoesia
mi domando chi è la madre mia

17
and anyway I'm not fish for your frying pan
fry and sauté others
I'm small and black
and not enough for your throat

18
you will have little time to say
a black shadow is advancing on the river
or all the time you want
if they fuck with you about the story of my eternity
don't believe the liars and the optimists
reclaim your liberty
of ending up in the canals and marshes

19
I feel like I will end uttering a holophrase
or I will return farther back
to babbling

20
honestly I can't say
that I'm a furious and confused dick
even if I lose my head too

21
poetry or nonpoetry
I wonder who my mother is

Stercoraria e nullatenente

1
non ti contristare
perché il vento viene da lo mare

2
stercoraria e nullatenente
invece di stritolare problemi impertinenti
me ne vado a dissotterrare stercora senza fumo

merda de vitello non fumat a lungo

3
corda corta ai birbanti
sennò incordano anche me
impigliata ai dati marginali
alle sedie impagliate

4
mi non son bìgoli e pan gratà
svaghezza per nessuno
non supplisco né risarcisco
e quando il fegato s'è fritto
chi non conta gli sghei
ha poco da magnà

5
morsi grossi e c'è poco da spolpare

6
che sconforto e soffocamento
cacciarsi in tutti i buchi
con o senza ismi

Destitute and Living in Dung

1

don't be sad
because the wind comes from the sea

2

destitute and living in dung
instead of chewing cheeky problems
I'm gonna go dig up a smokeless dunghill

veal guts non fumat for long

3

short cord to the rascals
otherwise they string me up too
wound up in fringe details
attached to straw seats

4

I'm not bigoli and breadcrumbs
leisure for no one
I don't ask for or offer refunds
and when the liver is fried
whoever doesn't count pennies
has little to eat

5

big bites and there's little to be stripped

6

what despair and suffocation
hiding in all the holes
with or without isms

7

in quest'aria trista e carestiosa
le parole intrappolano savi e matti
e nessuno si dimanda se li santi stanno ignudi

8

e se tu mi pisci
io ti caco
poeta senza pepe

9

se offendo prendo martello e incido il marmo
se ricevo offesa
scrivo sul ghiaccio e lo metto al sole

10

rido quando voglio
e piango quando posso

11

dietro la fortuna del romanzo e della poesia
non ci sarà mica una questione di misoginia?

12

per conto mio non riconosco altra signoria
e so che non perirai per i pericoli che temi
e sbronzo come sei di lessemi
ausculti il rumore del tuo ruminìo
finché maculando gentilezza
esci di casa mia armato contro il vuoto

13

se con gaudio non patisci fatica assai
lascia quest'arte sdesolata
e vai a ciapà sei sghei
prima che finisca a risata

7

in this sad and famished air
words trap the wise and mad
and no one asketh if the saints are naked

8

and if you piss me off
I shit on you
poet without pepper

9

if I offend I get a hammer and engrave the marble
if I get offended
I write on ice and put it in the sun

10

I laugh when I want
and cry when I can

11

behind the fortune of the novel and of poetry
is there not a question of misogyny?

12

as for myself I recognize no other rule
and I know you will not die for the dangers you fear
and drunk as you are on root words
you listen to the buzz of your slurred speech
until with spotty politeness
you leave my house armed against the emptiness

13

if in joy you do not suffer much fatigue
leave this desolate art
and go earn six coins
before it ends in laughter

14
si muore d'intossicamento e di febbre d'aria
t'hanno pigliato d'occhio ed è pigliata forte
guatatura combinatoria non allegra ventura

15
la tua incazzatura
è a giusta misura
se non sono chiacchiere

16
sono nell'acqua e muoio di sete

17
facciamo mano-manuzza
teniamoci stretti
contro lo malo vento tristo
e continuiamo la serenata

18
quando ti conviene
te ne stai in campana
tutto appartato
statuetta di santo paesano

14
you die of intoxication and of fever in the air
they took you under their eyes and took it hard
conjoining gazes not a happy venture

15
your anger
is at the right level
if they're not gossips

16
I'm in the water and dying of thirst

17
holding hands
let's hold tight
against the dark sad wind
and continue the serenade

18
when it suits you
you sit tight
all sequestered
statuette of a peasant saint

Del poesificio

1
lavorando a pasta e pastetta
tra campi semantici e geosinonimi
pensi che saliranno le azioni del poesificio?

2
e intanto ti attieni a verba generalia
quod non sunt impiccicatoria

3
se dici e sfingi fino allo sfinimento
perché non intrecci paglia?

4
segna quanto hai
quanto fai e sai
scava il pozzo
e porta l'acqua all'agrumeto

5
la lingua non serve soltanto a lappare
e non dire
chi disse, disse solo
        fu

6
meglio bocca aperta
che culo chiuso
a costo di mordersi la lingua
e battersi sul petto mea-cupla mea-culpa

chi non parla muore

In the Poetry Factory

1

working on dough and hanky-panky
between semantic fields and regional neologisms
do you think shares of the poetry factory will increase?

2

meanwhile you stick to verba generalia
quod non sunt impiccicatoria

3

if you say and play sphinx until exhaustion
why don't you weave straw?

4

mark how much you have
how much you know and do
dig the well
and bring the water to the citrus grove

5

the tongue is not only for lapping
and don't say
who said, only said
        it was

6

better an open mouth
than a closed ass
at the expense of biting your tongue
and beating your chest mea culpa mea culpa

the one who doesn't speak dies

7
zitto tu e zitta io
dovremmo fare i giocarelli dei bambini
le belle statuine madama do re?

8
a essere cucchiara di tutte le pentole
ti sconfondi di brodo soffritto e caponata
meglio conservarsi per una sola portata
lasciando ad altri la frittata

9
lasci la pentola come la trovi bogliente
ma vegnarà che il coperchio salta
e sì sarai dolente
che non saprai dire niente

10
rompi morfemi
o conta càntari all'ospedaletto

7
shut up and I'll shut up
must we play children's games
red light green light statues?

8
to be the master of all the pots
you mix yourself with broth and caponata
better to save it for one signature dish
leaving the omelet for others

9
you leave the pot when you find it boiling
but the lid will jump
and yes you will be sore
enough not to know how to say anything

10
break morphemes
or count chamber pots at the little country hospital

Coltellate di bellezza

1

corri al monte di pietà e spegna il modello vivente
nudo e infreddolito stringilo al petto
e lascia in pegno cotesta martoriata ripetitività

al senzapanni manca il pane

2

nessuno mi restituirà il tempo
che mi mangi a tradimento
rompisegni e leccacarte

e l'inchiostro non arriva al pennino
per cortezza di penna o fondezza di calamaio

3

e ricòrdati che i meglio colpi
sono sulla faccia
i meglio graffisegni sulla carta
non dimenticando il pugno allo stomaco

4

carichi fumo con la grinta junior
e ti pensi di fare sangue e latte con travaglio

fumo mi dài e fumo ti rimando

5

mi piacerebbe avere una casa a tre solai
e uscire ubriaca e insana dal fòndaco di millanterìa
facendo parole con gli angeli e i lampioni
che non ci sono più

Stabs of Loveliness

1

run to the pawnshop and turn off the living model
clutch him to your chest naked and cold
and leave as a pledge to that tortured monotony

the one without clothes lacks bread

2

nobody will give me back the time
that eats me treacherously
signbreakers and paperlickers

and the ink doesn't reach the nib
for the shortness of pen or depth of inkwell

3

and remember that the best blows
are on the face
the best scratch marks on paper
not forgetting the punch to the stomach

4

loads of smoke with minor grit
and you think to make blood and milk with suffering

you give me smoke and smoke I send back

5

I would like to have a three-story house
and leave drunk and insane from the foundry of swagger
making words with the angels and lampposts
that are no longer there

6

di fronte alla tua taccagnerìa senza punta né tacco
mi spingo a scippare chiodi coi denti
e mi mangio il fegato senza gusto né piacere

7

nuda
più nuda di così
si muore

8

starò o starraggio in compagnia tua
per rompimento di chiocche
per fare un po' di rumore . . .

preferisco occultare l'arte di accoltellare

9

mi rifiuto di stare sui trampoli
zuccherdosa e slavata
aspettando d'essere prosciugata

10

m'arrocco e non mi scastro
dove il pane è più salato
e lascio la melassa alle formìcole

11

confessi che ti spremi per farmi
e quando vai a tagliare il mazzo
puntualmente ti cade la regina di cuori
qualche altro intanto allustra parole
non sapendo fare scarpe

6

in front of your stinginess without beginning or end
I force myself to snatch nails with my teeth
and I eat my liver without relish or pleasure

7

naked
more naked than this
you die

8

I will stay or settle in your company
with the bother of blows
to make a bit of buzz . . .

I prefer to conceal the art of stabbing

9

I refuse to remain on stilts
sugared up and washed up
waiting to be dried up

10

where the bread is saltier
I castle myself and I don't unstick
and I leave the molasses to the ants

11

confess that you press yourself to get me
and when you go to cut the deck
the queen of hearts promptly falls out
meanwhile someone else polishes words
not knowing how to make shoes

12
mi pensavo di fare perciamento
e casco in buchi neri a ogni infuscamento

e comunque tròvami tu un altare senza croce
è più facile un pastore senza gregge

13
mi inviti a pasta e sarde
a pastiera di pasqua
e a ricotta salata
poi apri la bocca e dici cacca
pretendendo d'insegnare a spese d'altri

14
quand'è il caso
mi calo la visiera
e do coltellate di bellezza

12
I thought about making an aperture
and dropping into black holes with every darkening

and anyway find me an altar without a cross
a shepherd without a flock is easier

13
you invite me for pasta and sardines
for Easter cake
and for salted ricotta
then you open your mouth and say shit
expecting to teach at the expense of others

14
when it's time
I drop my visor
and drive stabs of loveliness

Sono questi i fiori

1
caldo di mani e freddo di capa
potresti fare un taglia-taglia
di fili snicchi e pupazzi snacchi
se ci mettessi un po' di penna
in questa storia di scrittura
ma camminando-camminando
te la vai toccando
e non sai più qual è l'occhio che ride

2
e di te diranno
è morto e va cantando

3
il forno roventa
la pizza s'avvampa
la pizia non c'è più
ricacciata dai forconi
e allora sgrìsola sega sbrega
e poi dimmi chi si storce e dà gomitate

4
e tròvala tu un'altra combinatoria come me
ladra e intrallazzara
che non ha denti e mozzica amara

sono questi i fiori

5
il caldo t'è entrato nel costato
io qua te metto
qua te lasso
e me ne vago a spasso
e come finisce finisce

These Are the Flowers

1
hot hands and cool head
you could try a snip-snip
of hidden threads and pushed-down puppets
if you put a little ink
to this paper history
but on and on
you go on tapping
and you don't know anymore which is the eye that laughs

2
and they'll say of you
he's dead and goes on singing

3
the oven scorches
the pizza glows
the priestess is gone
chased by pitchforks
and then shiver saw snatch
and now tell me who prods and pokes

4
and find another version someone like me
a thief and dealmaker
who doesn't have teeth and bites bitterly

these are the flowers

5
the heat has entered your chest
I put you here
here I leave you
and I'll be on my way
and how it ends it ends

non mi aggrada vederti confortato
con uno spicchio d'aglio

6

ma almeno getta un grido e non andare
a metterti sotto le anche di livide calliopi
che slebbrano e slabbrano
incapaci di tracciare recinti intorno al vuoto

7

io sottoscritta poesia
nasco per sorte mia
da parenti di primo o più lontano grado

pidocchi fanno pidocchi
le lire lirette
quattro e quattro non fanno sempre due
e forse c'entrerà la genotipìa

8

ti piglio a maleparole semplicemente perché
andato nel campo delle esercitazioni
non sai dare coltellate di verità
e intoni il miserère
mentre per le strade ci si scanna con la solita pietà

9

i meglio testi sono quelli che si fanno
impastando farina acqua e sale reale
come i maccheroni cavati col ferruzzo
mio bell'oste
e il conto è salato
pervolendo non pigliarla in culo per divozione

I don't like to see you comforted
with a clove of garlic

6
but at least scream and don't go
putting yourself under the hips of vengeful muses
who stretch and dissect
unable to erect fences around the void

7
I the undersigned poetry
I'm born to my fate
from relatives of first or distant degree

lice makes lice
money monies
four and four doesn't always make two
and maybe genetic makeup will matter

8
I curse you simply because
you left for the battlefield
you don't know how to drive stabs of truth
or sing songs of mercy
while on the streets we kill each other with the usual pity

9
the best verses are those that one makes
kneading flour water and real salt
like macaroni grooved with a cast-iron tool
my beautiful host
and the bill is expensive
even if I don't want to take it up the ass for devotion

10

scapricciata e scorchigliera
mi vanto di non essere nessuno
di grattare spezie sapori e aromi
al fondo dei tegami
per vedere chi arriva prima di lontano

11

sguarrare le parole
e farne vicoli angiporti angst angina
senza aggiunta di papaverina

12

bobba intruglio
smallazzo capitombolo
fattécchia schiamazzo
il catalogo è questo
e non ho nessuna voglia
di mettermi il cuore in pace

13

avvampo e non svampo
ingarzapelluta senza scampo
(scema-scema

10

wild and vagabond
I'm proud of being nobody
of scratching spices tastes and aromas
at the bottom of the pan
to see who arrives first from faraway

11

ripping apart the words
and making lanes angiporti anxiety angina
without the addition of papaverine

12

slop broth
falling tumble
magic cackle
this is the catalog
and I don't have any desire
to put my heart at peace

13

I blaze and don't flare
veiled in skin without escape
(dum-dum

Non è per vanto

1

tu di là io di qua
dopo questa rifottitura senza rinfrescamento
a leggere in un orto di carte con desfortuna

lèvati e non fare il lumacone che sbava

2

dopo i quarantatré malanni
c'imbarchiamo senza gallette
su gusci spicchi per mari spacchi

restano a terra i ladri accarezzati
(leccarsi la minchia come i cani?

3

e chi porta la notizia a casa
dopo averci appicciato l'olio la legna e la lanterna?
non t'impalano e l'anima te la fanno uscire dal culo

4

continuo ad avere l'acqua dentro casa
e tu baci le mani a chi se le merita tagliate

5

con le ali cadute
la bella fottuta struscia e striscia
dentro quattro metri quadri
e sai che scroscio fa

6

ho il gusto guasto
e il miele pare fiele

It's Not for Boasting

1
you over there me over here
after being screwed over without refreshment
reading in a paper garden with misfortune

scram and don't be a snail that drools

2
after the forty-three ailments
we board without biscuits
wedge-shaped shells for split seas

leaving the cherished thieves on land
(licking their dicks like dogs?

3
and who brings home the news
after having lit the oil the wood and the lantern?
they don't impale you and they force your soul out your ass

4
I still have water inside the house
and you kiss the hands of those deserving to be cut

5
with fallen wings
the beautiful fucker scuffs and streaks
inside four square meters
and you know what a roar it makes

6
I have a taste breakdown
and the honey seems bile

7
piangi con un occhio
(molto meglio non avere manco quello

8
girai l'erca e la merca
per raccontare i quarantatré giorni
dell'infausto festino
e mi ritrovo con i fogli stracciati
e senza riscaldamento
la lingua però . . . non è per vanto . . .

9
ti ripari sotto le grondaie
e domandi perché hai freddo e tremi

10
a me invece l'ultima scaglia
s'è infilata sotto un'unghia

11
non mi storco e non m'incrino
quando strigliata e pulita
mi porti in giro di cazzo in palazzo
e resti a mani vuote e occhi pieni

12
sono dolce e divento amara?

13
troppa mercanzia e nessun mercato
qua per te non luce la fiera
ti conviene smontare la tenda
dal regno dell'immaginario

7
cry with one eye
(much better to not even do that

8
circled the kneading trough and the market
recounting the forty-three days
of the inauspicious party
and I find myself with torn sheets of paper
and without heat
the language though . . . it's not for boasting . . .

9
you take shelter under the gutters
and ask why you're cold and shivering

10
but for me the last sliver
has slipped underneath a nail

11
I don't bend and I don't crack
when groomed and cleaned
you tease me for shit in the palace
and you're left with empty hands and full eyes

12
I'm sweet and become bitter?

13
too much merchandise and no market
here the fair doesn't pay off for you
you better take down the tent
from the realm of the imaginary

È un vecchio chiodo

1

mi infasci e sfasci
e così sono morta e sono in vita
fo il frutto e poi fiorisco

2

se vuoi metterla così
e insisti con l'ispirazione
non c'è problema
lei è la cocotte dei mediocri
aspettala anche tu
come l'aspettano trafficanti e impotenti
nei vicoli più deserti
o nelle piazze più affollate
ma non fare che di me si dica
che sono descaduta
io ti apro le porte del paese reale

3

sei morto spellato spelato
e vai vociando per le strade
ti getti a terra e sbavi
ti sberretti e svuoti

è un vecchio chiodo

4

stammi sotto e conta la tua pena
entrerai vuoto e uscirai pieno
sono granda e dispettosa
e dunque non chiamarmi femmina amorosa

It's an Old Nail

1

you bind me and break me
and so I'm dead and alive
I make fruit and then bloom

2

if you want to put it that way
and insist with ingenuity
it's not a problem
she's the streetwalker of mediocrity
you wait for her too
just like the traffickers and the helpless wait
in the most deserted alleys
or in the busiest piazzas
but don't let it be said about me
that I'm a fallen woman
for you I open the doors of a real country

3

you're skinned dead stripped
and go shouting through the streets
you throw yourself to the ground and drool
you remove your cap and lie bare

it's an old nail

4

stay under me and await your punishment
you'll enter empty and leave full
I'm big and spiteful
so don't call me an affectionate woman

5

ho solo figli per lo più assatanati
e non uno che sia disorganico e integrale

6

bella in vista e dentro trista
non raddrizzo minchiestorte e me ne vanto
tra lampi tuoni e vento

7

sei dentro lo specchio
e non puoi entrarci
a seminare nova semenza

8

fuggo di fronte alle amputazioni
per non ridurmi moncherino
e mi ritrovo di faccia sfregiatori con la scimitarra

9

catapuntiamo-scatapuntiamo
(non siamo scarabei
e facciamo palle

5
I only have children who are mostly crazy
and not fragmented or complete

6
a fair face and a foul heart
I don't straighten out crooked dicks and I boast of it
between lightning thunder and wind

7
you are inside the mirror
and can't enter it
to sow new seed

8
I run away from amputations
so I'm not reduced to a stump
I find myself facing slashers with scimitars

9
we blast-shitblast
(we're not beetles
and we make balls

Servizio d'attesa

1

sberrettato e sbrindellato
vai in pellegrinaggio dal santuario
delle frappole alle catracchie
dopo avere gettato a mare tutti i santi
il demonio strapiange e la madonna ride
ma per favore piglia la sedia
e siediti per l'orazione

2

tocchi gratti e togli onore
e pretendi rispetto tu e il tuo ron-ron-ronino
ma guarda che mi tocchi il nervo maestoso
col tuo sgocciolio nemmanco rugiadoso

3

fatti la fama e la cuccia e pensa a te
per la mia santonina non c'è febbre
e soprattutto non attacco il padrone
dove vuole l'asino

4

come mi tocchi
ti subisso di dissenteria
per navate labirinti portolani e così sia
vai con quella ruffiana de Melpòmene e spazia via
soggetto vuoto per oggetti perduti

5

in nome mio non si fanno né riffe
né lotterie di beneficenza
conserva questo vino che è vero
e diventerà aceto buono

Waiting Service

1

bareheaded and tattered
you go on a pilgrimage to the sanctuary
of jagged little tar pits
after having thrown all the saints into the sea
the devil wails and the madonna laughs
but please find a chair
and sit down for the prayer

2

you touch scratch and snatch the honor
and demand respect for you and your purr-purring
but look you also touch my majestic nerve
with your drippings not even dewy

3

build your fame and your den and think for yourself
with my wormseed there's no fever
and above all I don't tether the master
where he wants to put the donkey

4

the minute you touch me
I cover you with shit
through ships labyrinths maritime charts and so on
go with that Melpomene witch and be gone
empty subject for lost objects

5

don't make raffles
or charitable lotteries in my name
save this wine that's legit
and it will become good vinegar

6

ti metti di casa e poteca
in cortigli e imbrogli
manco per pane e companatico
ma io-poesia che c'entro
con tutta questa porcheria?

7

mai andato alla taverna
non scotti per sbronza né dài di stomaco
tra te e me c'è il ponte
che passa sulla vita senza doppi vetri

8

mi chiamo piritacchio
e faccio servizio d'attesa
stando mai in attesa
per servizi di inquaraquàcchio

9

e poi anche un cavallo s'inquarta
quando le mosche sono tante

6

you live for your family and house
among gossip and messes
not even making enough for bread and drippings
but what does I-poetry have to do
with all this trash?

7

never away at the tavern
you don't burn for hangovers or an upset stomach
there's a bridge between you and me
that goes through life without double glazing

8

my name is little farty
and I provide a waiting service
never standing at attention
for services of fuckery

9

and later a horse grows larger
when there are many flies

E venga un nuovo scorticatore

1
non potendo salire muri lisci
per punto de honor-puntiglio
portare al trotto le rumorose batterie
per le vie auguste di nostra terra

2
in faccia a stragi e contumelie
non ci servono nonne speranze
che sbrodettano

3
e venga un nuovo scorticatore
a trarre Marsia di sua pelle
piripacchio spockiano e spocchioso
che succhia con la bocca a cuore

4
come il padrone è padrone
perché ha torto e vuole ragione
così tu sei poeta
(Petrarca Petrarca
quanti guai

5
e se indovini «io travaglio e lei suda»
ti do quattro versi senza metronomo

6
tu ce l'hai
io ce l'ho
non nominare il mio invano

And a New Cheapskate Comes

1

unable to climb smooth walls
a point of privilege-honor
to lead the noisy drums to a trot
through the august streets of our land

2

in the face of massacres and insults
we don't need old biddies
who gossip

3

and a new cheapskate comes
to draw Marsyas out of his skin
kazoo Spockian and smug
who sucks with a heart-shaped mouth

4

how the master is the master
because he is wrong and wants to be right
so you're a poet
(Petrarch Petrarch
how many troubles

5

and if you guess "I work and she sweats"
I'll give you four verses without a metronome

6

you've got it
I've got it
don't name mine in vain

7

eppure il poeta sfortunato
o s'impicca o è martoriato

8

solo la seppia ha i figli in testa
e il padreterno fa figli crocifissi

9

carne venduta merce in ribasso
vuoi diventare come il santo del quadro
appeso al muro
e quattro di pappa cinque di nappa
metti a soqquadro comparati e baronie
e fai il soldo con la carta
nascondendo l'asso nella manica

7
nevertheless the unfortunate poet
is either hung or tortured

8
only the cuttlefish conceives children via the head
and the eternal Father makes crucified children

9
meat sold merchandise in decline
you want to become like the saint of the painting
hanging on the wall
and four of mush five of tuft
turn relatives and barons upside down
and make money with the card
hiding the ace up your sleeve

Corda bagnata in acqualanfa

1

non è sproloquio muto il mio
bersagliato da spifferate e ladrerie di sottobosco
mentre tu vai cantando mirtilli e mortelle

sproloquio per sproloquio
quest'anno sproloquiare è più che fottere
soprattutto tenendo per la cima corda bagnata
in acqualanfa

2

se dici saia saia sia
la meglio parola è quella che si dice
per non fare come il vacco
che ha la lingua grossa e non parla

3

e se non vuoi cantare (ne hai tutte le ragioni)
conta le sette spighe e i tre agnelli
i cavoli e i misteri gaudiosi

sognato fu l'altrui sogno

4

non entra mosca in bocca chiusa
non s'agitano moscerini dove non c'è vino

5

cambiano rime e ritmi
cadenze e scadenze
poemi e strutture
ma è sempre lo stesso e sempre stretto
il culo di chi comanda
con qualche rarissima eccezione

Noose Soaked in Orange Blossom Water

1

it's not a rambling speech mine's mute
pelted by tip-offs and low-life thieves
while you go on singing of blueberries and myrtle

rambling speech to rambling speech
this year ranting is better than fucking
especially holding onto the end of a noose soaked
in orange blossom water

2

if you say 'twill 'twill it will be
the best word is the one said
to avoid acting like a cow
that has a big tongue and doesn't talk

3

and if you don't want to sing (you have every reason not to)
count the seven ears and the three lambs
the cabbage and the joyful mysteries

someone else's dream was dreamed

4

a fly can't enter a closed mouth
gnats aren't excited where there isn't wine

5

rhymes and rhythms change
inflections and expirations
poems and structures
but the commander's ass
is always the same and always tight
with some very rare exceptions

6
ma non accettare che per potenza
si cachi in bocca alla ragione

7
parola mia
parola di poesia
perdurando lo scostumato parlamento
tra sinedrio e mercanti

è meglio essere pietra o quartara?

8
ti lasciano fare?
e lasciali dire

9
mentre che siamo coppia e stiamo qua
poesiamo
chissà se martedì poesia siamo

10
mi dispiaccio e m'incazzo
quando vedo che vuoi attaccare
padroni e minchioni
a rime e a minchiate

squaderni la risma e non combini niente

11
quando la minchia metterà unghie
potrai andare appresso ai tuoi nemici
e contargli le pedate

a questo punto è meglio voltarsi indietro
per trovare la strada e andare avanti

6
but don't accept the power
that shits in the mouth of reason

7
my word
word of poetry
an ongoing immoral parliament
between the great assembly and the merchants

is it better to be stone or terra-cotta pitcher?

8
do they let you be?
then let them talk

9
as long as we're together and here
we're poetrying
who knows if on tuesday we're poetry

10
I'm sorry and I'm pissed
when I see that you want to mash
masters and dumbasses
with rhymes and bullshit

you call out the kind and do nothing

11
when a dick grows nails
you may follow your enemies
and count their footsteps

at this point it's better to turn around
find the street and move on

12
alla poesia non c'è rimedio
chi ce l'ha se la gratta come rogna

13
nelle nostre campagne
dopo l'uso e l'abuso di diserbanti
è rimasto un passero solitario
che con arte incantatoria
piglia lanterne per lucciole

gli altri hanno cambiato contrada

14
niente illusioni
non hai virtù di guarire
scrofole col tocco

non fare come l'ochino di Cariddi
che in braghe de cerusico
dà aranciate e lupini
a un lumacone idropico

15
in tempo di carestia
tutti si gettano su una scarda di formaggio
e i formiconi rodono anco la scorza del sorbo

16
volta e rivolta
per mala perdizione ho mani e piedi legati
e sono morta e mortale

17
Dio c'è e anche il cacciucco

12
there's no remedy for poetry
those who have it scratch it like mange

13
in our countryside
after the use and abuse of herbicides
there remained a lone sparrow
that with an incantatory art
mistakes lanterns for fireflies

the others have changed sides

14
no illusions
you have no virtue to recover
from lesions with a touch

don't be like Charybdis's little seabird
who in the britches of a barber-surgeon
gives oranges and beans
to a watery slug

15
in times of famine
everyone throws themselves onto a hunk of cheese
and the ants also gnaw the rind of a sour fruit

16
turn and return
my hands and feet are tied by vile ruination
and I'm dead and mortal

17
God exists and so does the fish soup

18
crepa e sii grande

19
temperata bentemperata
stemperata e sventata
manco aceto per insalata

20
le vie del sublime sono infinite

18
drop dead and be great

19
tempered well-tempered
smashed and dashed
there's not even vinegar for the salad

20
the ways of God are endless

c'è in Asia un emiro emìono
che se la fa con un emitrago senza pizzo
ma vista la riprovazione dei parenti
si affidano ai versi e fanno emistichi

*

in Asia there's a wild-ass commander
that mates with a goat without a goatee
but given the disapproval of relatives
they rely on verses and make hemistiches

NOTES ON LATIN PHRASES

"I Said Nothing"

The line "culus perforatus non habet dominum" means "the pierced anus does not have a master."

The lines "de malo in malum / tornat et retornat / male dormit poeta qui non manducat" mean "from bad to bad / back and forth / the poet who does not eat sleeps badly."

The phrase "de lacte et pane bono / suam vaccam debet nutrire" means "good bread and milk / he must feed his cow" and is introduced in the poem by *manducare*, "to eat," which is the same verb in both Latin and Italian.

The line "planta de genista revertitur ad scopam" means "the broom plant turns back its branches."

The lines "de cultello ad pistolam / de cucina ad cessum / de ovo ad gallinam / de scala ad montem / de schola ad ecclesiam" mean "from knife to gun / from kitchen to toilet / from egg to hen / from ladder to mountain / from school to church."

"An Old Pleasure"

The line "croce de profundis et de sanctis" means "the holy and sacred cross." Insana uses this religious framework to comment on the cultural politics of twentieth-century Italy. Her diction alludes to various intellectuals, including the literary critic Francesco De Sanctis, whose populist views differed from the views of Pier Vincenzo Mengaldo mentioned in the previous line. Mengaldo advocated for a literary criticism informed by philology and style, while De Sanctis believed that art should be measured by the historical and social conditions of the writer. The philosopher Benedetto Croce is also implicated in the debate and represents the agnostic, anti-fascist, spirit-seeking aesthete.

"Destitute and Living in Dung"
The phrase "non fumat" means "don't smoke."

"In the Poetry Factory"
The expression "verba generalia / quod non sunt impiccicatoria" means "vague words / because they don't entail commitment" and is used in Sicily to point out when someone skirts obligations by speaking in an unclear or indirect manner. The Italian *da impiccio*, meaning "hindrance," "trouble," or "bother" is derived from *impiccicatoria*.
The phrase "mea culpa mea culpa" means "my fault my fault."

"These Are the Flowers"
The word "angiporti" means "alleys."

ACKNOWLEDGMENTS

My gratitude to the editors of the following journals, in which versions of these poems first appeared:

Massachusetts Review: "I Said Nothing" and "An Old Pleasure"
Paris Review: "Noose Soaked in Orange Blossom Water"

I am grateful to the Fondazione Ugo Da Como in Lonato del Garda for my translation residency and most especially to Giovanna Nocivelli and Giovanni Sciola.

Thank you to Andrea Brazzoduro, Kate Chandler, Elizabeth Harris, Anna Mauceri Trimnell, Susan McCabe, Steven Aaron Minas, Jan Minas, Lucia Senesi, Maria Luisa Theis, and William Theis.

Thank you to Srikanth "Chicu" Reddy, Rosa Alcalá, Douglas Kearney, and Katie Peterson for recognizing Jolanda Insana's fierce voice and talent. I want to thank Chicu and Katie, in particular, for their generous wisdom and insight.

Thank you to Alan Thomas, David B. Olsen, Lily Sadowsky, Adrienne Meyers, and the terrific team at the University of Chicago Press.

Finally, my deepest gratitude to Gian Maria Annovi and David St. John. Without these angels, no poetry exists.